AN INTRODUCTION TO THE FIVE PRACTICES OF EXEMPLARY LEADERSHIP

James M. Kouzes
& Barry Z. Posner

Pfeiffer
A Wiley Imprint
www.pfeiffer.com

Published by Pfeiffer
An Imprint of Wiley
989 Market Street
San Francisco, CA 94103-1741
www.pfeiffer.com

For additional copies/bulk purchases of this book in the U.S. please contact 800-274-4434.

Pfeiffer books and products are available through most bookstores. To contact Pfeiffer directly call our Customer Care Department within the U.S. at 800-274-4434, outside the U.S. at 317-572-3985, fax 317-572-4002, or visit www.pfeiffer.com.

Pfeiffer also publishes its books in a variety of electronic formats. Some content that appears in print may not be available in electronic books.

ISBN: 978-0-4705-9198-7

Acquiring Editor: Lisa Shannon
Director of Development: Kathleen Dolan Davies
Development Editor: Janis Fisher Chan
Production Editor: Dawn Kilgore
Editor: Rebecca Taff
Manufacturing Supervisor: Becky Morgan
Design: izles design

Printed in the United States of America

Printing   10 9 8 7 6 5 4 3 2 1

CONTENTS

Welcome

LEADERSHIP IS EVERYONE'S BUSINESS

In today's world there are countless opportunities to make a difference. There are opportunities to restore hope and renew meaning in our lives. Opportunities to rebuild a sense of community and increase understanding among diverse peoples. Opportunities to turn information into knowledge and improve the collective standard of living. Opportunities to apply knowledge to products and services, creating extraordinary value for the customer. Opportunities to pursue peace when so many wage war. Opportunities to use the tools of technology to weave a web of human connection. Opportunities to find a better balance in our always-on, 24/7/365 lives. Opportunities to provide direction and support during uncertain times.

As there has been in all times of change and uncertainty, there is a need for people to seize these opportunities and lead us to greatness. There is a need for leaders to inspire us to dream, to participate, and to persevere. This introduction to *The Five Practices of Exemplary Leadership*® offers you the chance to do just that—to take the initiative, to seize the opportunities, and to make a difference.

Since 1982, when we began our research, we've been fortunate to hear and read the stories of thousands of ordinary men and women who have led others to get extraordinary things done. The stories we've collected are not from the famous politicians or corporate CEOs who so often get the credit. They're not from the media celebrities or legendary entrepreneurs.

The people we've studied are your neighbors, your colleagues, and your friends. People just like you. These choices are intentional. Without them—and you—nothing great would ever get done. And if there's one singular lesson about leadership from all of the cases we've gathered it's this: **leadership is everyone's business**.

This is the truth that forms the foundation of The Five Practices Model. This is the truth that informs our selection of the stories we tell, the examples we give, and the activities we facilitate. We know that you can learn to become a better leader, and we know that you can make an even greater positive difference than you are now making.

Wanting to lead and believing that you can lead are the departure points on the path to leadership development. Stepping out there and exploring the territory, however, is the only way to learn, and that's how we've designed this introductory session. It's a voyage of self-discovery that begins with an expedition into your inner terrain and ends with your commitment to guide others along the path to distinction.

Welcome aboard, and have fun!

JIM KOUZES & BARRY POSNER

● ● ● ● ● ● ● ● ● ● ● ●

66 Our strength as humans and as leaders has nothing to do with what we look like. Rather, it has everything to do with what we feel, what we think of ourselves.... Leadership is applicable to all facets of life. 99

VERONICA GUERRERO,
WINNING EDGE RESEARCH

ORIENTEERING

Fundamentals

- Leadership is everyone's business.

- Leadership is a relationship.

- Leadership development is self-development.

- The best leaders are the best learners.

- Leadership development is not an event—it's an ongoing process.

- It takes practice—deliberate practice—to become a better leader.

- Leadership is an aspiration and a choice.

● ● ● ● ● ● ● ● ●

66 **Leadership opportunities are presented to everyone.... What makes the difference between being a leader and not is how you respond in the moment.** 99

MICHELE GOINS,
CHIEF INFORMATION OFFICER FOR
HEWLETT–PACKARD'S IMAGING
AND PRINTING GROUP

What if someone walked into this room right now and said...

"Hi, I'm your new leader."

What are the questions you'd want to ask that person?

Workshop Objectives

As a result of participating in this introduction to *The Five Practices of Exemplary Leadership*® session, you will be able to:

- Describe The Five Practices of Exemplary Leadership®.

- Name the essential qualities that people look for and admire in leaders and state the implications for your leadership.

- Identify your leadership strengths and areas of improvement based on your *Leadership Practices Inventory* self-assessment.

- Employ at least one method for improving your capacity to engage in each of The Five Practices.

- Make commitments on what you will do to contribute to getting extraordinary things done in your organization.

My Objectives:

_____

....

_____

....

_____

....

_____

....

Personal Best Leadership Experience

In preparing for this workshop, you wrote about your Personal Best as a leader. Take a few moments now to review your notes and get ready to tell your story. Be prepared to hear about some extraordinary accomplishments from your colleagues.

When you listen to your colleagues' stories, what behaviors, actions, and attitudes seem to be the keys to their leadership success?

....

....

....

What common leadership practices, actions, behaviors, or themes run through all the stories?

....

....

....

LEADERSHIP IS...

ORIENTEERING | PAGE 8

"THE ART OF mobilizing others TO want TO STRUGGLE FOR shared aspirations."

—JIM KOUZES AND BARRY POSNER

The Five Practices of Exemplary Leadership®

How do you get other people to follow willingly, especially when you set out across unknown territory? How do you mobilize other people to move forward together in a common purpose? How do you get others to want to get extraordinary things done?

We interviewed more than five hundred individuals, reviewed more than twelve thousand case studies, and analyzed more than a million survey questionnaires to find out what leaders do to make themselves leaders when performing at their best.

By studying times when leaders performed at their personal best, we were able to identify Five Practices common to most extraordinary leadership achievements.

When leaders are at their best, they:

1. Model the Way

2. Inspire a Shared Vision

3. Challenge the Process

4. Enable Others to Act

5. Encourage the Heart

The Five Practices of Exemplary Leadership®

1. MODEL THE WAY

- Clarify values by finding your voice and affirming shared ideals.

- Set the example by aligning actions with shared values.

....

....

....

....

....

....

....

....

....

....

2. INSPIRE A SHARED VISION

- Envision the future by imagining exciting and ennobling possibilities.

- Enlist others in a common vision by appealing to shared aspirations.

....

....

....

----

3. CHALLENGE THE PROCESS

- Search for opportunities by seizing the initiative and by looking outward for innovative ways to improve.

- Experiment and take risks by constantly generating small wins and learning from experience.

....

....

....

4. ENABLE OTHERS TO ACT

- Foster collaboration by building trust and facilitating relationships.

- Strengthen others by increasing self-determination and developing competence.

5. ENCOURAGE THE HEART

- Recognize contributions by showing appreciation for individual excellence.

- Celebrate the values and victories by creating a spirit of community.

The Leadership Practices Inventory

What does the LPI measure?

- The LPI was developed to validate Jim Kouzes' and Barry Posner's findings from their Personal Best Leadership case studies. The research data consistently shows that leaders who engage in the behaviors measured by the LPI are more effective and successful than those who do not.

- The LPI has thirty behavioral statements, six for each of The Five Practices. You and your observers indicated how frequently you engaged in those behaviors on a scale ranging from 1, meaning "almost never" to 10, meaning "almost always."

- The LPI provides information about you and your observers' perceptions of your leadership behaviors; it does not evaluate your IQ, leadership style, management skill, or personality.

- Research demonstrates that increasing the frequency with which you engage in the behaviors measured by the LPI—in other words, The Five Practices—will make you a more effective leader.

For more about the research, visit www.leadershipchallenge.com/go/research.

....

....

....

LPI Instructions

Please read each statement carefully and, using the rating scale on the right, ask yourself:

"HOW FREQUENTLY DO I ENGAGE IN THE BEHAVIOR DESCRIBED?"

- Be realistic about the extent to which you **actually** engage in the behavior.

- Be as honest and accurate as you can be.

- **Do not** answer in terms of how you would like to behave or in terms of how you think you should behave.

- **Do** answer in terms of how you typically behave on most days, on most projects, and with most people.

- Be thoughtful about your responses. For example, giving yourself 10s on all items is most likely not an accurate description of your behavior. Similarly, giving yourself all 1s or all 5s is most likely not an accurate description either. Most people will do some things more or less often than they do other things.

- If you feel that a statement does not apply to you, it's probably because you don't frequently engage in the behavior. In that case, assign a rating of 3 or lower. For each statement, decide on a response and then record it.

After you have responded to all thirty statements, go back through the LPI one more time to make sure you have responded to each statement. **Every** statement **must** have a rating.

THE RATING SCALE RUNS FROM 1 TO 10. CHOOSE THE NUMBER THAT BEST APPLIES TO EACH STATEMENT.

1. = Almost Never

2. = Rarely

3. = Seldom

4. = Once in a While

5. = Occasionally

6. = Sometimes

7. = Fairly Often

8. = Usually

9. = Very Frequently

10. = Almost Always

For each statement, decide on a response and then record the corresponding number in the box to the right of the statement.

LPI Questions (1–15)

1. I set a personal example of what I expect of others. ☐

2. I talk about future trends that will influence how our work gets done. ☐

3. I seek out challenging opportunities that test my own skills and abilities. ☐

4. I develop cooperative relationships among the people I work with. ☐

5. I praise people for a job well done. ☐

6. I spend time and energy making certain that the people I work with adhere to the principles and standards we have agreed on. ☐

7. I describe a compelling image of what our future could be like. ☐

8. I challenge people to try out new and innovative ways to do their work. ☐

9. I actively listen to diverse points of view. ☐

10. I make it a point to let people know about my confidence in their abilities. ☐

11. I follow through on the promises and commitments that I make. ☐

12. I appeal to others to share an exciting dream of the future. ☐

13. I search outside the formal boundaries of my organization for innovative ways to improve what we do. ☐

14. I treat others with dignity and respect. ☐

15. I make sure that people are creatively rewarded for their contributions to the success of our projects. ☐

LPI Questions (16–30)

16. I ask for feedback on how my actions affect other people's performance.

17. I show others how their long-term interests can be realized by enlisting in a common vision.

18. I ask "What can we learn?" when things don't go as expected.

19. I support the decisions that people make on their own.

20. I publicly recognize people who exemplify commitment to shared values.

21. I build consensus around a common set of values for running our organization.

22. I paint the "big picture" of what we aspire to accomplish.

23. I make certain that we set achievable goals, make concrete plans, and establish measurable milestones for the projects and programs that we work on.

24. I give people a great deal of freedom and choice in deciding how to do their work.

25. I find ways to celebrate accomplishments.

26. I am clear about my philosophy of leadership.

27. I speak with genuine conviction about the higher meaning and purpose of our work.

28. I experiment and take risks, even when there is a chance of failure.

29. I ensure that people grow in their jobs by learning new skills and developing themselves.

30. I give the members of the team lots of appreciation and support for their contributions.

LPI Scoring

INSTRUCTIONS

1. Transfer your ratings from the statements on the questionnaire to the blanks below. Please notice that the numbers of the statements are listed from *left* to *right*. Make certain that the number you assigned to each statement is transferred to the appropriate blank.

2. Add the columns and fill in the totals.

1. _____	2. _____	3. _____	4. _____	5. _____
6. _____	7. _____	8. _____	9. _____	10. _____
11. _____	12. _____	13. _____	14. _____	15. _____
16. _____	17. _____	18. _____	19. _____	20. _____
21. _____	22. _____	23. _____	24. _____	25. _____
26. _____	27. _____	28. _____	29. _____	30. _____

TOTAL:	TOTAL:	TOTAL:	TOTAL:	TOTAL:
Model the Way	**Inspire a Shared Vision**	**Challenge the Process**	**Enable Others to Act**	**Encourage the Heart**

What Do the Scores Mean?

Our research has shown that the higher your scores on the LPI, the more others perceive you as:

- Having a high degree of personal credibility

- Being effective in meeting job-related demands

- Being able to increase motivation levels

- Being successful in representing your group to upper management

- Having a high-performance team

- Fostering loyalty and commitment

- Reducing absenteeism and turnover and reducing stress levels

In addition, those working with you feel significantly more satisfied with your practices and strategies, more committed, and more powerful and influential.

Reflecting on Your LPI Self-Assessment

In which of The Five Practices are you the strongest? In which practice or practices could you use the most improvement? List two or three LPI items (behaviors) that you scored yourself highest and lowest.

1. ....

----

2. ....

----

3. ....

What other thoughts, questions, or observations do you have after considering your LPI self-assessment?

1. ....

----

2. ....

----

3. ....

Orienteering Summary

Think about where you are on your journey. If you were to leave the workshop now, what would you tell people back home is the most significant lesson you learned about yourself as a leader?

MODEL THE WAY

Model the Way

To model effectively, leaders must be clear about their guiding principles and then speak clearly and distinctly about what they believe. They also forge agreement about a set of common principles and ideas that make the organization unique and distinctive.

But eloquent speeches about personal values are not enough. Leaders stand up for their beliefs. They practice what they preach. They show others by their own example that they live by the values that they profess. Leaders know that, while their position may give them authority, it is their behavior that earns them the respect of their constituents. It is the consistency of word and deed that builds a leader's credibility.

MODEL THE WAY COMITTMENTS

Clarify values by finding your voice and affirming shared ideals.

Set the example by aligning actions with shared values.

Characteristics of an Admired Leader

Percentage of Respondents Who Selected the Characteristic as One of the Seven Qualities They Most Admire in a Leader

THIS
GROUP NORMS

THIS
GROUP NORMS

Ambitious
(aspiring, hardworking, striving)

_____ _____

Broad-minded
(open-minded, flexible, receptive, tolerant)

_____ _____

Caring
(appreciative, compassionate, concerned, loving, nurturing)

_____ _____

Competent
(capable, proficient, effective, gets the job done, professional)

_____ _____

Cooperative
(collaborative, team player, responsive)

_____ _____

Courageous
(bold, daring, fearless, gutsy)

_____ _____

Dependable
(reliable, conscientious, responsible)

_____ _____

Determined
(dedicated, resolute, persistent, purposeful)

_____ _____

Fair-minded
(just, unprejudiced, objective, forgiving, willing to pardon others)

_____ _____

Forward-looking
(visionary, foresighted, concerned about the future, sense of direction)

_____ _____

Honest
(truthful, has integrity, trustworthy, has character, is trusting)

_____ _____

Imaginative
(creative, innovative, curious)

_____ _____

Independent
(self-reliant, self-sufficient, self-confident)

_____ _____

Inspiring
(uplifting, enthusiastic, energetic, humorous, cheerful, positive about the future)

_____ _____

Intelligent
(bright, smart, thoughtful, intellectual, reflective, logical)

_____ _____

Loyal
(faithful, dutiful, unswerving in allegiance, devoted)

_____ _____

Mature
(experienced, wise, has depth)

_____ _____

Self-controlled
(restrained, self-disciplined)

_____ _____

Straightforward
(direct, candid, forthright)

_____ _____

Supportive
(helpful, offers assistance, comforting)

What Constituents Expect of Leaders

Four Characteristics of Admired Leaders

....

....

The four characteristics that constituents expect of leaders add up to what communications experts refer to as **source credibility**. According to those experts, a source of information is considered believable when he or she is considered to possess the following three characteristics.

Components of Source Credibility

....

Research has shown that people consistently select four characteristics to describe the leaders they would choose to follow.

Impact of Credibility on an Organization

When people perceive their managers to have high credibility, they are more likely to:

- Be proud to tell others they're part of the organization.

- Feel a strong sense of team spirit.

- See their own personal values as consistent with those of the organization.

- Feel attached and committed to the organization.

- Have a sense of ownership of the organization.

When people perceive their managers to have low credibility, they're more likely to:

- Produce only if they're watched carefully.

- Be motivated primarily by money.

- Say good things about the organization publicly, but criticize it privately.

- Consider looking for another job in tough times.

- Feel unsupported and unappreciated.

How do leaders earn credibility? What is credibility behaviorally?

_____ _____ _____ _____ _____ _____ _____

Clarify Values

Values are the moral judgments, responses to others, and commitments to personal and organizational goals that:

- Help us determine what to do and what not to do.

- Influence every aspect of our lives.

- Set the parameters for our decisions we make every day.

Credo Memo

FROM: _____

TO: _____

SUBJECT: _____

DATE: _____

I have written the following memo on the values
and principles I would like you to use in making
decisions and taking action during my absence.

....

....

....

....

....

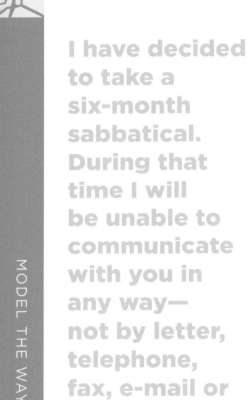

I have decided
to take a
six-month
sabbatical.
During that
time I will
be unable to
communicate
with you in
any way—
not by letter,
telephone,
fax, e-mail or
messenger.

Credo Memo Notes

Align Actions with Values

Here are some ways in which leaders demonstrate their values:

CALENDARS

How you choose to spend your time is the single clearest indicator of what's important to you. If you say something is important, then it had better show up on your calendar, on your meeting agendas, and in the places you go and people you see.

CRITICAL INCIDENTS

Chance occurrences and unexpected intrusions, which often occur during times of stress or change, bring into high relief questions of values. Critical incidents offer great opportunities to teach important lessons about appropriate norms of behavior.

STORIES

Stories are among the most important ways we pass along lessons from person to person, group to group, generation to generation. When someone says, "The moral of the story is…" you know he or she is about to communicate an important point. Leaders use stories to illustrate how values come to life in the organization. They can then serve as a kind of mental map that helps people know what is important and "how things are done around here."

LANGUAGE

Leaders choose their words carefully to make sure that people get the right message. They use metaphors—figures of speech in which a word or a phrase denoting one kind of idea is used in place of another—and analogies—words suggesting a resemblance in some ways between two things that are otherwise unlike—to enhance communication. And they ask questions to frame issues and set the agenda.

MEASUREMENTS

Measurement and feedback are essential to improved performance, so the outcomes and actions that are measured are the ones on which people focus. The LPI is also a measurement tool that helps you focus on a leader's critical behaviors.

REWARDS

The behaviors you reward, the people you recognize, and the accomplishments you celebrate send out signals about what matters to you. Make sure that, if you say a value is important, you tangibly and intangibly recognize performance that demonstrates the value.

Sample Values in Action Worksheet

CORE VALUE: CUSTOMER SERVICE

ACTION IDEAS

Calendar

- Answer customer services phones one morning per month.
- Visit client sites once a week.

Incidents

- The next time there is an unusual disruption in normal service, take on a frontline job to demonstrate that the customer comes first.
- Assign specific roles for staff members to take during service disruptions and have people practice these roles.

Stories

- Begin every staff meeting with customer stories, including both successes and learning opportunities.

Language

- Start referring to staff members as "associates" instead of as employees.
- Eliminate "subordinate" from your vocabulary. Eliminate "us/them" language from interdepartmental conversations.

Measurements

- Conduct a customer satisfaction survey.
- Determine the key leading indicators of your success and make them the key measures for the future.

Rewards

- Give a company-wide bonus for improving customer satisfaction rating.
- Set up an Applause! Bulletin Board for every location.

Values in Action Worksheet

CORE VALUE: _____

ACTION IDEAS

Calendar
-
-
-

Incidents
-
-
-

Stories
-
-

Language
-
-
-

Measurements
-
-
-

Rewards
-
-
-

Model the Way
Module Summary

Clarify values by finding your voice and affirming shared ideals.

Set the example by aligning actions with shared values.

Where are you on your journey to become a better leader?

- -

. . . .

- -

What are the two most important things you learned about the practice of Model the Way?

1. . . . .

- -

. . . .

2. . . . .

- -

. . . .

How clear are you about the values and guiding principles that govern your decisions and actions at work?

- -

. . . .

- -

. . . .

INSPIRE A SHARED VISION

Inspire a Shared Vision

There is no freeway to the future, no paved highway from here to tomorrow. There is only wilderness, uncertain terrain. There are no road maps, no signposts.

Like explorers, leaders have their skills and experience to prepare them. Leaders look forward to the future. They gaze across the horizon of time, imagining the opportunities that are in store once they and their constituents arrive at their destination. They have a sense of purpose and a desire to change the ways things are. Their clear vision of the future pulls them forward.

But leaders know that they cannot command commitment, only inspire it. They know that vision is a dialogue, not a monologue. They share their dreams so that others can understand and accept them. They learn about their team members' dreams, hopes, and aspirations and forge unity of purpose by showing them how the dream is for the common good. They communicate their passion through vivid language and expressive style.

INSPIRE A SHARED VISION COMITTMENTS

Envision the future by imagining exciting and ennobling possibilities.

Enlist others in a common vision by appealing to shared aspirations.

Definition of a Vision

A vision pulls people forward. It projects a clear image of a possible future. It generates the enthusiasm and energy to strive toward the goal.

IDEAL (a high standard to aspire to)

Visions are about hopes, dreams, and aspirations. They're about making a difference. They tell us the ennobling purpose and greater good we are seeking.

UNIQUE (pride in being different, an identity)

Visions are about the extraordinary. They are about what makes us distinctive, singular, and unequaled.

IMAGE (a concept or mental picture made real or tangible through descriptive language)

Word pictures, metaphors, examples, stories, symbols, and similar communication methods all help make visions memorable.

FUTURE-ORIENTED (looking toward a destination)

Visions describe an exciting possibility for the future. They stretch our minds out into the future and ask us to dream.

COMMON GOOD (a way people can come together)

Visions are about developing a shared sense of destiny. Leaders must be able to show others how their interests are served and how they are a part of the vision in order to enlist others in it.

A vision is an **IDEAL** and **UNIQUE IMAGE** of the **FUTURE** for the **COMMON GOOD**.

Breathe Life into Your Vision of the Future

Draw a "mind map" to illustrate one of your themes.

1. Select one of the themes you associate with your future.

2. Write your theme in the circle in the middle of the page.

3. Illustrate your theme with word pictures by making all the associations you can with that theme—things, sounds, images, feelings, people, places—anything that comes to mind.

Inspire a Shared Vision Module Summary

Envision the future by imagining exciting and ennobling possibilities.

Enlist others in a common vision by appealing to shared aspirations.

What are the two most important things you learned about the practice of Inspire a Shared Vision?

1. ....

....

....

2. ....

....

....

How clear are you about the important themes and the higher-order values that give your life and work meaning and direction? About those of your constituents?

....

....

....

....

....

....

....

CHALLENGE THE PROCESS

Challenge the Process

Challenge is the opportunity for greatness. Leaders welcome opportunities to test their abilities. They look for innovative ways to improve their work and their organization.

Leaders venture out. They are willing to step in to the unknown. They know that innovation comes more from listening than from telling. They seek and recognize good ideas and challenge the system to get those ideas adopted.

Great leaders are great learners. They know that risk taking involves mistakes and failure, so they treat the inevitable disappointments as learning opportunities. They are willing to experiment and take risks in order to find new and better ways of doing things. Leaders also create safe environments in which others can learn from their failures as well as their successes.

CHALLENGE THE PROCESS COMITTMENTS

Search for opportunities by seizing the initiative and by looking outward for innovative ways to improve.

Experiment and take risks by constantly generating small wins and learning from experience.

One Leader Who Took the Challenge

Outsight

Where do good ideas come from? What are some ways you can use outsight—to search for opportunities and innovative ideas outside your team, organization, or industry?

....

....

....

....

....

....

....

Get out of the box.

Take Risks and Learn from Mistakes

Rules for building and maintaining a climate of trust

#1. You have to keep working on trust and never take it for granted.

#2. Sometimes trust breaks down. When it does, see Rule #1.

....

....

....

....

....

Helping People Take Risks and Learn from Mistakes

What generalizations would you make about making mistakes and creating a learning environment?

. . . .

. . . .

. . . .

How can you create an environment in which people learn from the inevitable mistakes of doing something new?

. . . .

. . . .

. . . .

One Hop at a Time

What are all the little things that the leader did to make progress?

Small Wins

Small wins create a pattern of winning that attracts people who want to be allied with a successful venture.

Leaders identify the place to get started and begin by modeling action. Breaking big, even overwhelming problems into small, manageable chunks is an important aspect of creating small wins. Leaders work hard at finding ways to make it easy for the team to succeed.

What makes small wins so successful in creating momentum for change?

Why use small wins?

Key Actions for Generating Small Wins

- Break it down. Break big problems down into small, doable pieces.

- Make a model. Create a small-scale version of what you're trying to do so you can see whether it will work.

- Keep it simple. Your visions should be grand, but keep your actions as simple as possible.

- Do the easy parts first. Help the group discover that they can do it.

- Accumulate YESES. Ask for agreement to do the first thing, then the second, then the third, etc.

- Experiment. Try, fail, learn, then try again.

- Give feedback. Let people know how they are doing.

- Celebrate. When you reach milestones, take the time to congratulate one another.

Challenge the Process
Module Summary

Search for opportunities by seizing the initiative and by looking outward for innovative ways to improve.

Experiment and take risks by constantly generating small wins and learning from experience.

What are the two most important things you learned about the practice of Challenge the Process?

1. ....

....

....

2. ....

....

....

Where can you look for creative, innovative ideas for addressing your challenges?

....

....

....

....

....

....

....

....

ENABLE OTHERS TO ACT

Enable Others to Act

Leaders don't travel alone. Leaders know that the team effort to make grand dreams become reality requires solid trust and strong relationships. Leaders foster collaboration. They nurture self-esteem in others and make them feel strong and capable. Leaders make sure that when they win, everybody wins.

Leaders make it possible for others to do good work. They build teams with spirit, cohesion, and a true sense of community. Leaders involve others in making plans and decisions, and develop collaborative goals and cooperative relationships.

Leaders strengthen and develop others by sharing power and information, and by giving others visibility and credit. As coaches and teachers, they give people challenging tasks, support them with the tools they need to be successful, and clear obstacles from their paths.

ENABLE OTHERS TO ACT COMITTMENTS

Foster collaboration by building trust and facilitating relationships.

Strengthen others by increasing self-determination and developing competence.

• • • • • • • • • • • • • •

❝ The best way for me to give power to other people… is to allow creativity and freedom to explore new ideas and ways of thinking. ❞

JILL CLEVELAND,
FINANCE MANAGER OF APPLE, INC.

Powerful Times, Powerless Times

Think of a time or times when you felt **powerful** as a result of what someone said or did.

Describe what the person said and/or did. Be as specific as you can.

....

....

....

Think of a time or times when you felt **powerless** as a result of what someone said or did.

Describe what the person said and/or did. Be as specific as you can.

....

....

....

What is the impact on your productivity and your
morale when someone does or says something
that makes you feel powerful?

. . . .

. . . .

What is the impact on your productivity and your
morale when someone does or says something
that makes you feel powerless?

. . . .

. . . .

What are the implications for you as a leader?
Share your reasoning.

. . . .

. . . .

. . . .

Powerful Times

- Behaviors that make people feel powerful are enabling, and those that make people feel powerless are disabling.

- Feeling powerful is likely to bring out the best, most positive, most committed energy and performance.

- Making people feel capable and valued is at the heart of trust—the essential ingredient in people's willingness to take risks that can drive extraordinary results.

What have you said or done recently to enable your constituents by making them feel powerful?
Cite examples and be as specific as you can. Describe WHEN you actually did or said WHAT to enable WHOM.

....

....

What have you said or done recently that might have been disabling to your constituents and made them feel powerless? Be specific.

....

....

What barriers get in the way of enabling others?
What could you do to remove or reduce these barriers?

....

....

How One Leader Strengthens Others

LEADER'S ACTIONS

LEADER'S CONTRIBUTIONS

LEADER'S RELATIONSHIPS

WHAT CAN YOU DO?

Develop Cooperative Goals and Roles

Shared goals and shared roles bind people together in collaborative pursuits. As individuals work together and recognize that they need each other in order to be successful, they become convinced that everyone should contribute and that, by cooperating, they can accomplish the task successfully.

Leaders should think about what they can do to **foster collaboration in a given situation**—how they can structure the situation so that each member of the team must contribute to the success and so that no one wins unless everyone wins.

Note any initial action ideas that occur to you for improving the frequency with which you engage in those behaviors.

With your increased awareness about leadership, which six leadership behaviors would you like to be able to engage in more often?

Behavior number and name:

_____

....

Action ideas:

_____

....

Behavior number and name:

_____

....

Action ideas:

_____

....

Behavior number and name:

_____

....

Action ideas:

_____

....

Behavior number and name:

....

Action ideas:

....

Behavior number and name:

....

Action ideas:

....

Behavior number and name:

....

Action ideas:

....

Enable Others to Act Module Summary

Foster collaboration by building trust and facilitating relationships.

Strengthen others by increasing self-determination and developing competence.

What are the two most important things you learned about the practice of Enable Others to Act?

1. ....

....

....

2. ....

....

....

What's the relationship between the level of the challenge and the level of your competencies and skills within my team?

....

....

....

....

....

....

....

ENCOURAGE THE HEART

Encourage the Heart

Getting extraordinary things done in organizations is hard work. People become exhausted, frustrated, and disenchanted. Leaders Encourage the Heart of their team members to carry on. They inspire others with courage and hope.

To keep hope and determination alive, leaders show genuine appreciation for individual excellence. They express pride in the accomplishments of their team, and they make everyone feel like everyday heroes.

ENCOURAGE THE HEART COMITTMENTS

Recognize contributions by showing appreciation for individual excellence.

Celebrate the values and victories by creating a spirit of community.

Most Meaningful Recognition Activity

Think about one of the most meaningful recognitions you have ever received. It can be related to any part of your life—work, family, school, or community. What was the recognition? Why did you receive it? What made it so meaningful for you? Be as specific as you can.

- -

. . . .

- -

. . . .

- -

. . . .

What are some of the common elements that you heard from your colleagues' most meaningful recognition stories?

- -

. . . .

- -

. . . .

- -

. . . .

• • • • • • • • • • • • • •

66 If everyone is doing a great job, what's the problem in letting them know that? 99

LINDSAY LEVIN,
WHITES GROUP CHAIRMAN

The Essentials of Encourage the Heart

EXPECT THE BEST

Successful leaders have high expectations of themselves and of others. People frequently step up to higher levels of performance when expectations are high. Leaders bring out the best in others by making sure that people know what is expected of them and by encouraging them to be their best.

PERSONALIZE RECOGNITION

Leaders pay attention to remarkable achievements as well as achievements that are relatively small in scope, yet are personal breakthroughs, and recognize them. A cornerstone of meaningful recognition is that it is perceived as personal. For example, leaders tell stories with vivid details that reinforce **why** a person is being recognized. Personalized recognition lets people know they are valued as unique individuals and that their leaders have a thoughtful and personal interest in their accomplishments.

CREATE A SPIRIT OF COMMUNITY

Leaders not only recognize individual excellence, but they celebrate team values and victories. Celebrating together creates a heightened sense of community, belonging, and inclusion. It sends a message that everyone benefits when great things occur and reminds people of the enormous potential of what can be accomplished together.

BE PERSONALLY INVOLVED

You cannot delegate affairs of the heart. As a leader you must search for examples of people doing things right. You must be willing to look people in the eye and tell them thank you. You must be personally involved with people, so you know when they are worthy of special recognition or need reassurance or guidance when they have tough work to do. Your acts of encouragement send very clear messages about the importance and legitimacy of what people do.

Encourage the Heart
Module Summary

Recognize
contributions
by showing
appreciation
for individual
excellence.

Celebrate
the values
and victories
by creating
a spirit of
community.

What are the two most important things you learned about the practice of Encourage the Heart?

1. ....

....

....

2. ....

....

....

Which of your team members would really benefit from more recognition? How would you personalize it?

....

....

....

....

....

....

....

COMMITTING

Committing

Every exceptional leader is an exceptional learner. Leadership development is an ongoing process that requires practice.

Many leadership skills can be learned successfully in the classroom, but we also learn from other people and from experiences. We must take advantage of every opportunity to practice our skills. We may fail, but we will learn from our mistakes.

Worksheet: Identifying My Goals

1. Review the notes you have made in this workbook and think about the insights you've had from the discussions and activities. Then select ONE of The Five Practices on which you want to focus your leadership development during the next thirty days (short-term, immediate actions you can take right after the workshop) and over the next ninety days (longer-term actions that require some preparation).

Practice to focus on:

- -

A useful template for thinking about your goals follows:

"In [time period]**, I will** [improve, increase, decrease, or eliminate _____] **so that** [describe payoff for self and organization]. **My success will be measured by** [describe tangible or observable outcomes]."*

- -

· ·

- -

· ·

- -

*Reprinted from *The Six Disciplines of Breakthrough Learning* (p. 91) by C. Wick, R. Pollock, A. Jefferson, and R. Flanagan. Published by Pfeiffer, An Imprint of Wiley, 2006.

2. **Identify your short-term and long-term goals for improving the leadership practice you have chosen.** Think about why you selected the particular goals and decide what specific actions you will take to achieve them.

SHORT-TERM GOALS (WITHIN THIRTY DAYS):

GOAL

REASONS FOR SELECTING

ACTIONS FOR ACHIEVING

LONG-TERM GOALS (WITHIN NINETY DAYS):

GOAL

REASONS FOR SELECTING

ACTIONS FOR ACHIEVING

Making Your Commitment

1. **Do a "reality check" of your development plans: Are they clear?** Do they make sense? Are there any additional ideas or suggestions that you might not have considered?

....

----

2. **Make a promise to your colleague that you will take these actions.**

3. **Schedule at least two in-person or telephone meetings during which you will discuss what each of you did, what happened, what you learned, and what you will do next.**

First meeting date and time (in about thirty days):

....

Second meeting date and time (in about ninety days):

....

Commitment partner's name

- -

Telephone number:

- -

E-mail address:

- -

Commitment partner's signature:

- -

Your Leadership Journey

We wish you continuing joy and success on your leadership journey!

We demonstrate our commitment to becoming a better leader—or to doing anything, for that matter—when we do three things:

- Freely choose actions.

- Go public with what we're going to do.

- Make it hard for ourselves to back out of our commitment to take those actions.

That's what you've done in this module. You have freely chosen goals you want to accomplish and actions you're going to take to achieve them. You made a public statement to at least one other person about what you're going to do. And you've made it harder to back out of your commitment by signing your commitment statement and arranging a time to talk about what you've done.

But the real test of your commitment comes when you leave *The Leadership Challenge® Workshop*. The true test is whether you "Do What You Say You Will Do" back in your organization. Your personal credibility will be strengthened the moment you take that first action step to apply what you've learned here.

JIM KOUZES

BARRY POSNER

● ● ● ● ● ● ● ● ● ● ● ● ● ● ●

66 **The real dividing line is passion. As long as you believe what you're doing is meaningful, you can cut through fear and exhaustion and take the next step.** 99

ARLENE BLUM,
PH.D. IN BIOPHYSICAL CHEMISTRY,
AVID MOUNTAIN CLIMBER

What's Next?

Because effective leadership development is not an event but an ongoing process, we have designed a full range of resources to support leaders in continuing their development in The Five Practices following *The Leadership Challenge® Workshop*. These include:

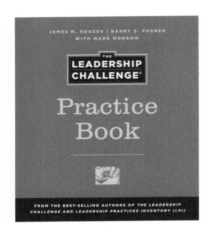

THE LEADERSHIP CHALLENGE PRACTICE BOOK

Helping leaders to actively use and improve their leadership skills in each of The Five Practices every day, the Practice Book guides leaders in daily activities to practice back on the job, and includes worksheets and grids for logging practice activities.

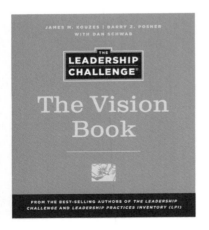

THE LEADERSHIP CHALLENGE VISION BOOK

This focused resource guides leaders through the process of developing and delivering their teams' vision messages and building their own and their teams' skills as visionaries.

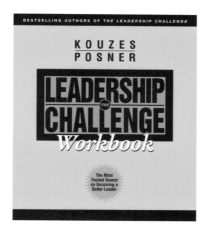

THE LEADERSHIP CHALLENGE WORKBOOK

This workbook is a hands-on guide for leaders to apply The Five Practices to a project of their choice, furthering their abilities to lead others to get extraordinary things done.

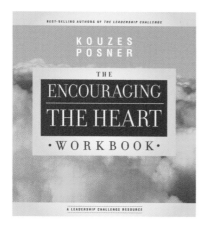

THE ENCOURAGE THE HEART WORKBOOK

For leaders seeking intense development in the fifth practice, Encourage the Heart, this self-study workbook provides detailed information and activities on mastering the four essentials of Encourage the Heart that will help them become more caring and credible leaders.

THE LPI

In this session you completed the LPI-Self. If you are ready to hear some valuable feedback, consider taking the LPI-360 assessment, available at www.lpionline.com. This web-based tool provides leaders with valuable feedback from managers, co-workers, direct reports, and others who have direct experience with the leader.

ABOUT THE AUTHORS

About the Authors

Jim Kouzes and Barry Posner are co-authors of the award-winning and best-selling book, *The Leadership Challenge*. This book was selected as one of the Top 10 books on leadership of all time (according to *The 100 Best Business Books of All Time*), won the James A. Hamilton Hospital Administrators' Book-of-the-Year Award and the Critics' Choice Award from the nation's book review editors, was a *BusinessWeek* best-seller, and has sold over 1.8 million copies in more than twenty languages.

Jim and Barry have co-authored more than a dozen other leadership books, including *A Leader's Legacy*—selected by *Soundview Executive Book Summaries* as one of the top thirty books of the year—*Credibility: How Leaders Gain It and Lose It, Why People Demand It*—chosen by *Industry Week* as one of its year's five best management books—*Encouraging the Heart*, *The Student Leadership Challenge*, and *The Academic Administrator's Guide to Exemplary Leadership*. They also developed the highly acclaimed *Leadership Practices Inventory* (LPI), a 360-degree questionnaire for assessing leadership behavior, which is one of the most widely used leadership assessment instruments in the world. More than four hundred doctoral dissertations and academic research projects have been based on the Five Practices of Exemplary Leadership® model.

Among the honors and awards that Jim and Barry have received are the American Society for Training and Development's (ASTD) highest award for their Distinguished Contribution to Workplace Learning and

Performance; Management/Leadership Educators of the Year by the International Management Council (this honor puts them in the company of Ken Blanchard, Stephen Covey, Peter Drucker, Edward Deming, Frances Hesselbein, Lee Iacocca, Rosabeth Moss Kanter, Norman Vincent Peale, and Tom Peters, who are all past recipients of the award); and named among the Top 50 Leadership Coaches in the nation (according to *Coaching for Leadership*).

Jim and Barry are frequent conference speakers, and each has conducted leadership development programs for hundreds of organizations, including Apple, Applied Materials, ARCO, AT&T, Australia Post, Bank of America, Bose, Charles Schwab, Cisco Systems, Community Leadership Association, Conference Board of Canada, Consumers Energy, Dell Computer, Deloitte Touche, Dorothy Wylie Nursing Leadership Institute, Egon Zehnder International, Federal Express, Gymboree, Hewlett-Packard, IBM, Jobs DR-Singapore, Johnson & Johnson, Kaiser Foundation Health Plans and Hospitals, L. L. Bean, Lawrence Livermore National Labs, Lucile Packard Children's Hospital, Merck, Mervyn's, Motorola, NetApp, Northrop Grumman, Roche Bioscience, Siemens, Standard Aero, Sun Microsystems, 3M, Toyota, the U.S. Postal Service, United Way, USAA, Verizon, VISA, and The Walt Disney Company.

JIM KOUZES

Jim Kouzes is the Dean's Executive Professor of Leadership, Leavey School of Business, at Santa Clara University. Not only is he a highly regarded leadership scholar and an experienced executive, but *The Wall Street Journal* has cited him as one of the twelve best executive educators in the United States.

In 2006 Jim was presented with the Golden Gavel, the highest honor awarded by Toastmasters International. Jim served as president, CEO, and chairman of the Tom Peters Company from 1988 through 1999, and prior to that led the Executive Development Center at Santa Clara University (1981–1987). Jim founded the Joint Center for Human Services Development at San Jose State University (1972–1980) and was on the staff of the School of Social Work, University of Texas. His career in training and development began in 1969 when he conducted seminars for Community Action Agency staff and volunteers in the war on poverty effort. Following graduation from Michigan State University (B.A. with honors in political science), he served as a Peace Corps volunteer (1967–1969). Jim also received a certificate from San Jose State University's School of Business for completion of the internship in organization development. Jim can be reached at **jim@kouzes.com**.

BARRY POSNER

Barry Posner is professor of leadership at Santa Clara University (Silicon Valley, California), where he has received numerous teaching and innovation awards and served as dean of the Leavey School of Business for twelve years (1996–2009). An internationally renowned scholar and educator, Barry is author or co-author of more than a hundred research and practitioner-focused articles.

He currently serves on the editorial review boards for *Leadership and Organizational Development*, *Leadership Review*, and *The International Journal of Servant-Leadership*. Barry is a warm and engaging conference speaker and dynamic workshop facilitator. Barry received his baccalaureate degree with honors from the University of California, Santa Barbara, in political science; his master's degree from The Ohio State University in public administration; and his doctoral degree from the University of Massachusetts, Amherst, in organizational behavior and administrative theory. Having consulted with a wide variety of public- and private-sector organizations around the globe, Barry currently sits on the board of director of EMQ Family First. He has served previously on the board of the American Institute of Architects (AIA), Junior Achievement of Silicon Valley and Monterey Bay, San Jose Repertory Theater, Public Allies, Big Brothers/Big Sisters of Santa Clara County, the Center for Excellence in Nonprofits, Sigma Phi Epsilon Fraternity, and several start-up companies. Barry can be reached at **bposner@scu.edu**.